OUR FIVE S

Sight

Popcorn

Sally Morgan

Explore the world with **Popcorn** - your complete first non-fiction library.

Look out for more titles in the **Popcorn** range. All books have the same format of simple text and awesome images. Text is carefully matched to the pictures to help readers to identify and understand key vocabulary.
www.waylandbooks.co.uk/popcorn

Published in 2013 by Wayland
Copyright Wayland 2013

Wayland
Hachette Children's Books
338 Euston Road
London NW1 3BH

Wayland Australia
Level 17/207 Kent Street
Sydney NSW 2000

Editor: Nicola Edwards
Designer: Robert Walster
Picture researcher: Shelley Noronha
Series consultant: Kate Ruttle
Design concept: Paul Cherrill

British Library Cataloguing in Publication Data
Morgan, Sally
  Sight - (Popcorn. Five senses)
  1. Sight - Juvenile literature
I. Title
612.8'4
ISBN: 978 0 7502 7858 4

10 9 8 7 6 5 4 3 2 1

Printed and bound in China

Wayland is a division of Hachette Children's Books,
an Hachette UK Company
www.hachette.co.uk

Photographs:
Cover: © Corbis; title page © David Gray/Reuters/Corbis; p2 Joey van Dun/istock; p4 Bananastock/Jupiter Media/ImagePick; p5 Denis Pepin/ Shutterstock; p6 Joey van Dun/istock; p7 Ellen Martorelli/Getty Images; p8 (l) Johanna Goodyear/ Shutterstock, (r) T-Design/Shutterstock; p9 Martyn f. Chillmaid; p10 © David Gray/Reuters/Corbis; p11 © Corbis; p12 Susanna Price © Dorling Kindersley; p13 Dmitry Pistrov/ Shutterstock; p14 Matthew Luzitano/ Shutterstock; p15 Vadim Koziovsky/ Shutterstock; p16 Nick Hawkes/Ecoscene; p17 Darren Green/ Shutterstock; p18 photoaloja/ Shutterstock; p19 Huib Theunissen/Shutterstock; p20 Martyn f Chillmaid; p21 altrendo images/Getty Images; p22 AFP/Getty Images; p23 Martyn f. Chillmaid

Contents

Seeing the world

We use our two eyes to see. Sight is one of our five senses. We use our senses to find out about our surroundings.

Our world is full of light and colour.

4

As soon as you wake up in the morning, you open your eyes. What do you see as you look around?

Which fruits can you see in this picture?

Our five senses are sight, hearing, touch, smell and taste.

Our eyes

Look at your eyes in a mirror. Can you see the dark spot in the middle of each eye? This is called the pupil.

eyelid

eyelashes

pupil

iris

We blink about 12 times every minute to keep the surface of our eyes clean.

The coloured part of the eye is called the iris. Most people have irises that are blue, grey, green, hazel or brown.

What colour are your irises?

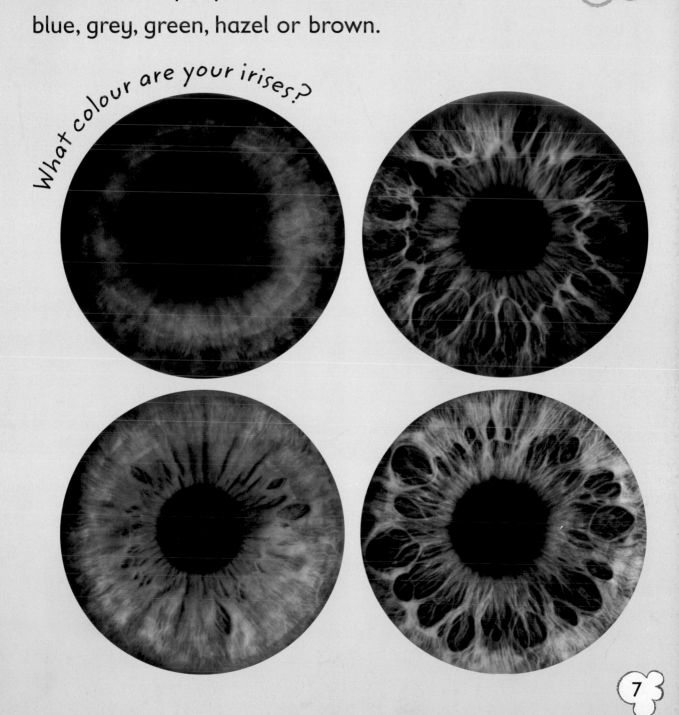

How do we see?

We need light to see. Light passes through the pupil to the back of the eye. There, a part of the eye called the retina detects the light. Then it sends a message to the brain.

Look at the difference in the size of the pupil in these two eyes.

In dim light the pupil is large, so lots of light enters the eye. In bright light the pupil is small to stop too much light entering.

In bright light we protect our eyes by wearing sunglasses.

Judging distance

Close one eye. Try picking up an object in the middle of the floor. Now pick it up with both eyes open. Which was easier?

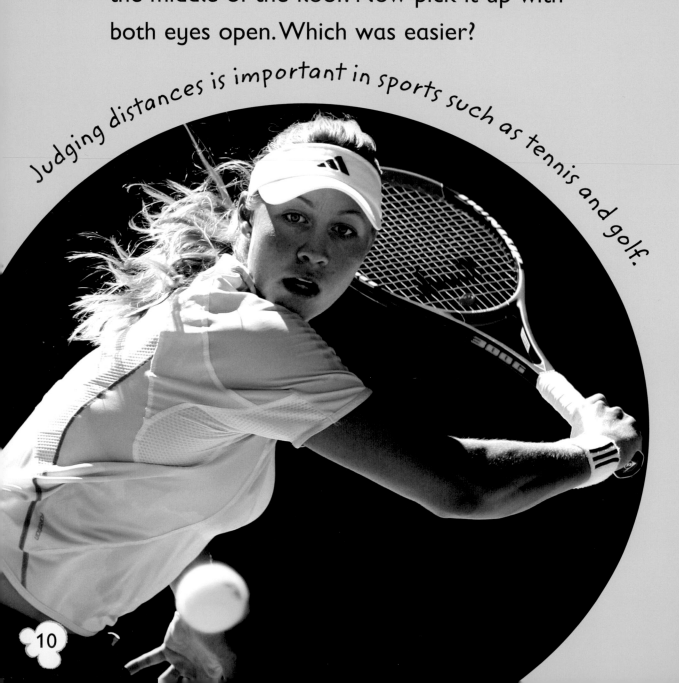

Judging distances is important in sports such as tennis and golf.

Our eyes work together so we can judge how far away an object is. This helps us to pick up objects, play sport and carry out tasks.

This boy is using his eyes to judge how far he needs to hit the golf ball.

Seeing all around

Put your arms out wide to your sides.
When you look straight ahead, you can see
your arms out of the corner of your eyes.

See if you can
spot coloured
cards placed at
the edge of
your vision.

Our eyes are
very good at
detecting movement
at the edge of
our vision.

We can see things in front of us, but nothing behind us. Many animals have eyes on the sides of their head so they can see in front and behind.

A horse's eyes are on the side of its head.

Seeing in colour

People can see in colour, but many animals see only in black and white and shades of grey. However, we can only see colours when there is plenty of light.

At night, in dim light, we cannot see colours.

People who are colourblind have difficulty seeing the difference between red and green colours.

A colourblind person cannot see the number 5 in this photo.

More boys are colourblind than girls.

15

Look out!

Bright colours, such as red and yellow, are easy to spot. People use these colours in warning signs to alert us to danger.

This yellow sign warns people to keep away from electricity lines.

DANGER!
OVERHEAD
ELECTRIC
POWER LINES

Animals use warning colours, too. Many poisonous animals are brightly coloured to warn other animals to stay away.

The brightly coloured poison arrow frog is one of the deadliest animals in the world.

👁 Animal eyes

Some animals, such as bears and rhinos, have poor eyesight. Others, such as owls and cheetahs, have very good eyesight. Many animals have eyes like our own, but some look very different.

Snails have eyes on the end of their tentacles.

Insect eyes are made up of lots of tiny
eyes that work together. These eyes
are good at detecting movement.

A fly's huge eyes give it excellent sight.

Problems with sight

Many people do not have perfect sight. They have to wear glasses or contact lenses to see far away objects or to read.

Our eyes must be checked regularly to make sure we can see clearly.

Blind people are unable to see. Some were born blind but others lose their sight through illness or in an accident.

Blind people use their other senses to find out about their surroundings.

Your sense of sight

Your eyes can play tricks on you. Look at these lines.
Which line looks longer?

Now measure each horizontal line with a ruler.
What do you notice?

Look at this picture. Do the dots look as if they are moving?

Now choose one of the patterns and stare at the centre of it.
What happens?

Find your blind spot

Ask a friend to stand about 10 metres away from you. Cover one eye and walk very slowly towards them, looking at their face. Suddenly, their face will disappear.

This happens because you have a blind spot. There is a particular point at the back of the eye that cannot detect any light. When light lands on this point you do not see anything. Normally, you do not notice this because you see through two eyes.

Glossary

blind spot part of the eye where there are no light detectors

brain the control centre of the body, found inside the head

colourblind unable to see certain colours

iris the coloured part of the eye that surrounds the pupil

pupil a hole in the centre of the eye that lets light pass through

retina the part of the eye that detects light

senses functions of the body through which we gather information about our surroundings

Index